Livonia Public Library
CARL SANDBURG BRANCH #21
30100 W. 7 Mile Road
Livonia, Mich. 48152
248-893-4010

MEET THE GREATS

Barack OBAMA

TIM COOKE

www.garethstevens.com. For a free color catalog of all our high-quality books, call toll free 1-800-542-2595 or fax 1-877-542-2596.

Cataloging-in-Publication Data

Names: Cooke, Tim.
Title: Barack Obama / Tim Cooke.
Description: New York : Gareth Stevens Publishing, 2019. | Series: Meet the greats | Includes glossary and index.
Identifiers: LCCN ISBN 9781538225738 (pbk.) | ISBN 9781538225721 (library bound)
Subjects: LCSH: Obama, Barack–Juvenile literature. | Presidents–United States–Biography–Juvenile literature.
Classification: LCC E908.C66 2019 | DDC 973.932092 B–dc23
NEED CIP

Published in 2019 by
Gareth Stevens Publishing
111 East 14th Street, Suite 349
New York, NY 10003

Copyright © 2019 Gareth Stevens Publishing

For Brown Bear Books Ltd:
Editorial Director: Lindsey Lowe
Managing Editor: Tim Cooke
Children's Publisher: Anne O'Daly
Design Manager: Keith Davis
Designer and illustrator: Supriya Sahai
Picture Manager: Sophie Mortimer

Concept development: Square and Circus / Brown Bear Books Ltd

Picture crediits: Front cover: Character artwork Supriya Sahai. Interior: AP: Ron Edmonds 22; Chicago Tribune: Chris Sweda 43t; Department of Defense: 21, 42; Dreamstime: Jose Gill 30, Joshua Wanyama 28; Getty Images: 29t, Keystone 15t; Library of Congress: 24b; Obama for America: 8, 9, 10, 18; Reuters: 40; Rex Features: 41; Robert Hunt Library: 14b, 15b; Shutterstock: Cheryl Casey 31, stock_photo_world 35t; Text Publishing: 25; Thinkstock: Peterspito 11, marchello74 12, 19, fotoguy22 20; Topfoto: Picturepoint 13; whitehouse.org: 23, 32, 38, Samantha Appleton 33, Pete Souza 34b, Chuck Kennedy 35b, Sonya Herbert 38.

Character artwork © Supriya Sahai
All other artworks Brown Bear Books Ltd

Brown Bear Books has made every attempt to contact the copyright holders.
If anyone has any information please contact licensing@brownbearbooks.co.uk

All rights reserved. No part of this book may be reproduced, stored in a retrieval system, or transmitted in any form or by any means, electronic, mechanical, photocopying, recording, or otherwise, without the prior written permission of the copyright holder.

CPSIA compliance information: Batch #CS18GS. For further information contact Gareth Stevens, New York, New York at 1-800-542-2595.

Contents

Introduction 4
Hawaiian Upbringing 6
   Feature: African American Heritage 14
Law and Civil Rights Politics 16
   Feature: Best-selling Author 24
The First Black President 26
   Feature: The First Family 34
Defending a Legacy 36
Timeline 44
Glossary 46
Further Resources 47
Index 48

Introduction

In 2009, Barack Obama became the first black president of the United States. He was also one of the youngest presidents.

The son of a white American mother and a Kenyan father, Barack was born and raised in Hawaii. After becoming a lawyer, he worked as a community organizer in Chicago before entering politics as a Democrat. He served in the Illinois Senate before becoming a US senator. Barack also became a best-selling author.

As the 44th president, Barack served two consecutive terms from 2009 to 2017. During that time, he worked successfully to improve a weak economy with low growth and high unemployment. His other achievements included introducing affordable health care—nicknamed Obamacare—for many uninsured Americans, and locating and killing the most wanted terrorist of the modern age, Osama bin Laden. When Barack Obama left office in January 2017, he had one of the highest approval ratings of any outgoing president.

Hawaiian
UPBRINGING

Barack Obama overcame obstacles and accomplished many things before becoming president of the United States.

Barack Hussein Obama II was born on August 4, 1961, in Honolulu, Hawaii. Neither of his parents were from the state. They met when they were studying at the University of Hawaii. Barack's mother, Stanley Ann Dunham, was originally from Kansas. She had moved with her parents to Hawaii. Barack's father, Barack Obama Sr., came from Kenya in East Africa. He belonged to the Luo people and had herded goats as a boy. Ann and Barack Sr. fell in love and decided to marry in 1961. At the time, marriage between white and black people was still illegal in many states.

MEET THE GREATS: BARACK OBAMA

QUICK FACTS
- Barack had an African father and an American mother, and grew up in Hawaii and Indonesia.
- Barack became interested in African American history as a high school student.

Barack's parents met at the University of Hawaii.

ON THE MOVE

In 1963, when Barack was two years old, his parents split up. They divorced in 1964. Barack Sr. moved 5,000 miles (8,000 km) to study at Harvard, Massachusetts. Barack was 10 years old when he saw his father again.

Young Barack and his mother lived with Ann's parents. Barack called them Gramps and Toot (*tutu* means "grandmother" in Hawaiian). The family called Barack "Barry" or "Bar." While his mother was busy with her university studies in anthropology, Barack's grandparents taught him the values of independence and honesty they had learned growing up in the Midwest.

A SECOND MARRIAGE

In 1967, Barack's mom remarried. His new stepfather was one of his mother's fellow students, Lolo Soetoro. Lolo came from Indonesia, a large island nation in the Pacific Ocean. That same year, Ann and Barack moved with Lolo to live in Jakarta, the Indonesia capital.

In 1971, Ann took Barack back to Hawaii to visit with his grandparents. He stayed there with Gramps and Toot when his mom returned to Indonesia. Barack's dad came to visit from Kenya. He stayed a month, and the father and son became close, although young Barack was initially horrified at the idea that someone he hardly knew could tell him what to do. When Barack Sr. left, it was the last time Barack would see him. His father was killed in a car crash in Kenya in 1982.

Barack Jr. was mainly brought up by his grandparents in Hawaii.

Barack found his teenage years difficult. Was he Barry or Barack? Was he Christian or Muslim, like his stepfather Lolo? Was he white like his mom or black like his dad? As he wrestled with these questions, his grades fell. Barack knew he had to do something. He started to read about the achievements of famous African Americans to help give meaning to his life.

COLLEGE YEARS

In 1979, Barack left Hawaii and moved to Los Angeles, California. There he spent two years studying at Occidental College, nicknamed Oxy.

As a teenager, Barack asked himself many questions about his identity.

Studying at Columbia brought Barack into contact with some of the poorest areas of New York City.

While he was at Oxy, Barack finally decided that he wanted to be known as Barack and not Barry. At the end of his sophomore year, he transferred to Columbia University in New York City. At last, he was working hard and getting good grades.

Columbia's campus was close to Harlem, where many poor African American families lived. As Barack explored the city, he saw the differences that existed in living conditions between rich and poor. Deciding that he wanted to work to change things, he majored in political science.

THE NEXT STEP

Barack graduated in 1983 and moved to Chicago, Illinois, to help poor African Americans. He got a job as a community organizer, working with local churches to rebuild communities that had suffered since the local steel plants had closed down. Barack's job was to solve any problems people faced, from getting a landlord to make repairs to an apartment to making the streets safer. Barack was soon making a real difference to people's lives. However, he realized that the best way to help the poor was through the law.

Barack moved to Chicago in 1983. It has remained his home ever since.

Barack's Kenyan relatives belonged to the Luo people.

AFRICAN FAMILY

Barack applied to one of the best law schools in the country, Harvard Law School in Boston, Massachusetts. He was accepted, but before starting law school, he decided to go to Kenya to meet his late father's family. Barack Sr. had married four times, so Barack had lots of half-brothers and sisters and aunts and uncles to meet. His paternal grandmother told him many stories about his father. For the first time, Barack really understood his Kenyan heritage—and he was very proud of it.

African American HERITAGE

In his late teens, Barack decided to learn as much as he could about African Americans who had helped to shape the United States.

His mother was interested in American history and passed the interest on to her son. Barack read about the **civil rights** movement of the 1960s, and leaders such as Martin Luther King Jr. and Malcolm X. He was fascinated by the different approaches the two men took toward civil rights. Malcolm X thought violence was sometimes necessary and that African Americans would live better as a separate nation. King believed passionately in using **nonviolence** to achieve results. He thought that white and black Americans should live together.

Martin Luther King Jr. addresses a rally in Washington, DC, in 1963.

FEATURE: AFRICAN AMERICAN HERITAGE

In the 1980s, South Africa was strictly divided on racial grounds.

At college, Barack became convinced that people of all races deserved the same rights. He became involved in the movement to end **apartheid** in South Africa.

Until 1994, a policy of apartheid, or separateness, ensured that black South Africans lived as second-class citizens, without political or social rights. Barack campaigned to end apartheid. He invited guest speakers to his colleges and gave speeches himself.

For the first time, Barack realized that he had the ability to move people with his words.

Students in the United States and around the world protested for the end of apartheid in South Africa.

15

Law and Civil Rights
POLITICS

The law changed Barack's life forever. He met his future wife at a law firm and embarked on a career in the law.

*I*n the summer of 1988, Barack returned from five weeks in Kenya and started at Harvard Law School. He was now 27 years old. Barack remained at Harvard until 1991. While there, he became president of the prestigious *Harvard Law Review*. The journal is published eight times a year, with legal articles written by law students. Barack was the first African American to be elected as the *Review*'s president. In 1989, Barack took a summer job at a Chicago law firm. His adviser there was a smart young lawyer named Michelle Robinson.

Barack and Michelle on their wedding day in 1992.

GETTING MARRIED

Michelle made quite an impression on Barack, although they later recalled that he made less of a first impression on her! By the time Barack went back to school in the fall, however, the couple had fallen in love. After graduating in 1991, Barack decided to make his home in Chicago with Michelle and took a job in a law firm. In 1992, he started to teach evening classes in law at the University of Chicago. That October, he and Michelle got married at the Trinity United Church of Christ on the South Side of Chicago.

A NEW FAMILY

Michelle worked full-time as a lawyer and, like Barack, she worked as a community organizer. She also worked for the Mayor's Office and in the University of Chicago Hospitals. On weekends, the couple spent time with Michelle's family, the Robinsons. They were the type of close-knit family Barack had never really known. His own family was scattered across the world.

Barack and Michelle both worked in the community in Chicago.

A POLITICAL CAREER

In 1992, Barack started working in local politics. Chicago had 400,000 African Americans who were not registered to vote. Barack started a volunteer program that helped 150,000 African Americans register. In 1993, his success led to him being named on a list of "40 under Forty" most influential people in Chicago. In 1996, he decided to run for public office. At age 35, he was ready for his next step.

The Illinois State Capitol in Springfield.

THE SENATE

In 1996, Barack won a seat on the Illinois senate. He wanted to clean up Illinois politics, which he felt were corrupt. He also wanted to improve health care for people who could not afford health insurance. Barack now worked in the state capital of Springfield while Michelle worked in Chicago. Barack could only go home on weekends. After Michelle gave birth to a daughter, Malia, in 1998, Barack tried to get home more often.

In 2000, Barack ran for a seat in the US House of Representatives. Michelle advised him against running because his opponent, Bobby Rush, had held the seat since 1993 and was very popular. She was proved right when Barack lost, but this didn't stop Barack. The couple had their second daughter, Sasha, in 2001.

In the fall of 2002, Barack gave a speech opposing the approaching war in Iraq. He was one of the few elected officials in the country to argue against the war. Once the war started, he supported US troops and their **allies**, although he still thought the war was a mistake. He promised to raise the issue when he ran for the US Senate in 2004.

Barack spoke out against sending US troops to Iraq.

Barack makes his speech at the Democratic National Convention.

STRIKING THE RIGHT NOTE

The Democratic **primary** in Illinois in March 2004 chose Barack to run for a seat in the US Senate. That July, the Democratic candidate for president, John Kerry, picked Barack to give the **keynote address** at the Democratic National Convention in Boston. The convention confirmed Kerry's nomination as the presidential candidate.

Barack was still unknown outside of Illinois, but not for much longer. Millions of Americans watched his keynote speech on television. Viewers liked his message that if people worked together, America could become an even better country.

A US SENATOR

In November 2004, Barack won his seat in the US Senate with 70 percent of the vote. As the only African American in the Senate and, at 43, one of the youngest senators, he received a lot of media attention. Barack arrived in the Senate vowing to make the federal government more open and accountable. He also worked for affordable health care and better schools and housing.

After serving just two years as a senator, Barack announced in February 2007 that he was going to run for president in the 2008 election. People were stunned. Not only did he have relatively little experience in national government, he was also very young. How was he going to finance his election campaign?

The official photograph of Barack when he was elected to the US Senate.

Best-selling AUTHOR

From an early age, Barack read widely. As a teenager, he read political biographies to help him understand the world better.

Even as president, Barack tried to read for an hour every evening. As well as **nonfiction**, he read novels and **biographies** because he wanted to understand the world from other people's points of view. Like another president, Abraham Lincoln, Barack also turned to writing books himself. While working as a community organizer, he had kept a journal and written short stories. He was inspired by speeches such as Lincoln's 1863 Gettysburg Address and Martin Luther King's 1965 civil rights speech, "I Have a Dream."

Barack studied the works of other political authors such as Abraham Lincoln.

FEATURE: BEST-SELLING AUTHOR

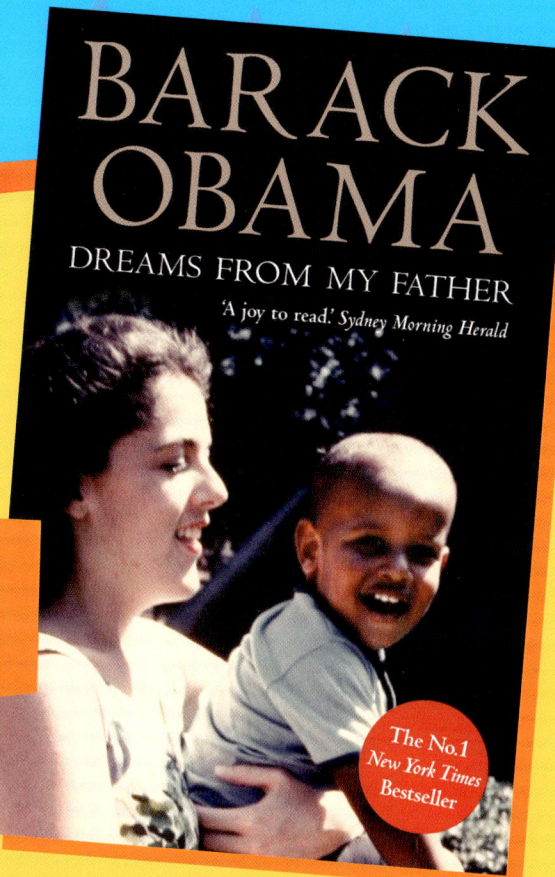

The cover of Barack's first book featured a photograph of him with his mother, Ann.

In 1995, Barack's book *Dreams from My Father*, was published. It has sold more than two million copies. The book explored Barack's search for identity as a young man. He followed up this best seller with two more books. He wrote *The Audacity of Hope* (2006) while he was a Senator. The title came from his speech at the Democratic Convention in 2004. While president, Barack wrote *Of Thee I Sing: A Letter to My Daughters* (2010), in which he told the stories of 13 great Americans —from Abraham Lincoln to the social worker Jane Addams. When he left the presidency in 2017, Barack planned to write his presidential **memoirs**.

The First Black PRESIDENT

In 2008, Barack Obama defeated his Republican opponent, Senator John McCain, in the presidential election.

When Barack announced that he would run to become Democratic candidate for president in early 2007, few people thought he would win. In June 2008, he won the nomination by defeating former First Lady Hillary Clinton in the primaries. During the late fall, Barack became more and more popular. Thousands attended his rallies. His campaign used social media to raise over half a billion dollars, the largest sum ever raised by a candidate for public office. Rather than relying on major **donors**, Barack reached out to many people who gave a few dollars each.

CHANGE IS COMING

On November 4, 2008, Barack defeated the Republican candidate, John McCain, in the presidential election. Barack won more votes than any candidate in history. In his acceptance speech, he said, "Tonight, because of what we did on this date, in this election, at this defining moment, change has come to America." Many Americans wanted change. The Republican Party had been in power since 2001. The United States was in the middle of a **recession** and the economy had collapsed. Many Americans lost their jobs, and when they could no longer repay their **mortgages**, they lost their homes. Barack promised to help.

Supporters at a rally celebrate Obama's election win.

Barack took office in the middle of an economic recession.

TO THE WHITE HOUSE

On January 20, 2009, Barack Obama was sworn in as the 44th president of the United States. The crowd stretched for 2 miles (3.2 km), the largest-ever crowd for an **inauguration**. The only sadness for Barack was that his mother and grandparents were not there to witness the event. His mom had died of cancer in 1995, and his beloved Toot passed away just two days before election day.

Barack surprised people when he made Hillary Clinton Secretary of State.

GETTING TO WORK

One of Barack's first jobs was to fill his cabinet. He decided the best person for the job of Secretary of State, the person in charge of US foreign policy, was his former rival, Hillary Clinton.

There was a lot of work to do. First, Barack had to address the country's economic problems. A famous bank, Lehman Brothers, had gone bankrupt in 2008. It was feared more banks would quickly follow. Barack introduced plans to stop the banks from failing. He also made plans to help the struggling auto industry, and to help people who were in danger of losing their homes through not being able to afford to pay their mortgages.

Barack's policies helped to stabilize the economy in the short term by making money available to the banks. In the long term, he turned around the economy by creating millions of new jobs.

SOCIAL ISSUES

Barack also continued to address the social issues that had concerned him as a community worker in Chicago. At the top of his list was making health care affordable for more Americans. Around 45 million people had no medical insurance. Barack wanted to pass a law that gave all Americans the chance to receive medical care, no matter what their income. Nicknamed "Obamacare," the program faced stiff opposition from Republicans in Congress. Despite this, Barack's plan became law on March 23, 2010.

Barack's attempts to change health care faced protests from Americans opposed to government interference in citizens' lives.

In October 2009, the Nobel Committee announced that Barack had won the Nobel Peace Prize for his efforts to improve international **diplomacy**. Barack was only the fourth US president to have been awarded the prize.

THE WAR ON TERROR

In foreign affairs, one of Barack and Hillary Clinton's priorities was the **war on terror**. US troops were fighting Islamic **extremists** in Afghanistan and Iraq. On May 1, 2011, Barack went on TV to tell Americans that US **special forces** had killed Osama bin Laden. Leader of the al-Qaeda terror group, bin Laden had masterminded the attacks on America on September 11, 2001.

Barack and his senior advisors watch the operation to kill Osama bin Laden.

Barack had ordered a team of US Navy SEALs to raid a compound in Pakistan where US intelligence agencies had discovered that bin Laden was hiding. The raid was successful, and the world's most wanted man was dead. The president also fulfilled a long-held promise when he withdrew American troops from Iraq in 2011.

MICHELLE'S ROLE

A key individual during Barack's first term was Michelle Obama. When Barack told his wife that he wanted to run for the presidency, she was reluctant. She did not want to uproot the family and move to Washington, DC. However, when she saw how much the presidency mattered to Barack, she decided to support him. Once in the White House, Michelle turned her attention to promoting the education of girls not just in America, but globally. She also supported healthy eating and exercise. She turned part of the White House lawn into a vegetable patch.

Michelle Obama (in red) watches children plant vegetables.

The First FAMILY

When Barack moved into the White House in 2008, his family went, too. His daughters, Malia and Sasha, were then ten and seven years old.

For eight years, the two girls grew up in a home with 132 rooms! To keep life as normal as possible, Michelle told White House staff not to clean the girls' rooms or make their beds. The girls had to do their own chores. They went to school in Washington, DC.

The Obama family in the White House in 2011.

FEATURE: THE FIRST FAMILY

Michelle speaks at an event for the "Let Girls Learn" program that she launched as First Lady.

As First Lady, Michelle was busy. She attended functions with Barack and also had her own causes to support. Michelle's mom, Marian Robinson, moved into the White House to help out with the girls—she was like a First Grandma! This helped make sure the move to Washington was not too hard for the girls. The family lived in their own apartment in the White House, so they could have privacy as the girls grew up.

To complete the First Family, the Obamas decided to get a dog. In 2009, they were given a Portuguese Water Dog they named Bo. A second Portuguese Water Dog, Sunny, joined the family in 2013.

Bo had his own official portrait photograph.

35

Defending a LEGACY

Barack decided he needed a second term in office to complete his ambitious plans. He stood for reelection in 2012—and won.

Barack's second term in office was frustrating. He had issues he wanted to address, such as gun control and **climate change**, but in 2010 the Republicans had won control of the House of Representatives. The Republican majority limited the president's powers to pass new legislation. His biggest regret was his failure to pass legislation to limit gun ownership following a series of high-profile shootings. He had more success internationally. After decades of hostility between the United States and Iran and Cuba, Barack worked with both countries to improve relations.

MEET THE GREATS: **BARACK OBAMA**

QUICK FACTS
* Barack was reelected for a second term in 2012.
* He was unable to pass some of the laws he cared about most passionately.

Barack takes the oath as president at his second inauguration.

SECOND TERM

In November 2012, Americans once again voted for their new president. Barack ran against the Republican candidate, Mitt Romney. Barack won 51.1 percent of the popular vote, making him the first president since Dwight Eisenhower in 1956 to win 51 percent of the vote twice. President Obama got right back to work.

LGBT RIGHTS

In his second inauguration speech, Barack reaffirmed his belief that everyone should be treated equally in the eyes of the law, regardless of their **sexual orientation**.

Barack supported laws to give equal rights to LGBT (lesbian, gay, bisexual, and transgender) people. In 2010, during his first term in office, he had introduced legislation to allow gay and lesbian people to serve in the military. During his second term, he fulfilled his ambition to make same-sex marriage legal. The Supreme Court ruled in its favor in 2015. To celebrate the ruling, the White House was lit up in the rainbow colors of the LGBT movement.

The White House illuminated in rainbow colors.

FOREIGN AFFAIRS

After the 1959 Cuban Revolution, the United States broke ties with its island neighbor, Cuba. On July 1, 2015, President Obama announced that diplomatic relations between the two countries would resume. He became the first sitting president to visit the island since 1928. Another foreign success was persuading Iran in the Middle East to stop trying to develop nuclear weapons. The agreement was signed in 2015 after two years of negotiations.

Meanwhile, a new organization replaced al-Qaeda as the leading terrorist threat. Known as ISIS, the terrorists fought in Syria and Iraq and carried out attacks across the Western world.

Barack and his family visit Havana, Cuba, in a rainstorm.

ISIS terrorists took control of large parts of Syria and Iraq.

Barack sent troops back to Iraq and announced air strikes against ISIS in neighboring Syria. The conflict continued through his second term, but by 2017, it was clear that ISIS was in retreat.

A BOOMING ECONOMY

During Barack's two terms, almost 10 million jobs were created. The impact of the 2008 recession had been reduced by steps to stimulate the economy. These measures included tax increases on the wealthy and tax cuts for poorer Americans, higher unemployment benefits, and the reduction of the federal budget **deficit**. However, Barack's attempts to remove **tariffs** on trade with 11 nations around the Pacific Ocean were blocked by Congress.

CLIMATE CHANGE

Barack was convinced that one of the biggest threats facing not just the United States but the whole world was climate change. Human activity was making the atmosphere warmer, with severe effects such as increased rains and flooding. Barack worked to reduce carbon emissions and also US dependence on imported oil. In 2015, the United States and 193 other countries, including China, signed the Paris Agreement to limit **global warming**. The United States is the world's second largest polluter after China. The signed agreement committed countries to reducing greenhouse gases, a major contributor to global warming.

Rescuers in Houston, Texas, in floods caused by Hurricane Harvey in 2017.

A Barack supporter displays her ticket for his final address in her hat.

LEAVING OFFICE

Barack's second term ended on January 20, 2017. During his farewell speech in Chicago, he said, "America is a better, stronger place than it was when we started." As a best-selling author, Barack's memoirs of his White House years were eagerly awaited. He and Michelle also set up a foundation to carry out work for the causes in which they strongly believe.

Traditionally, former presidents stay out of politics. However, following violence at a white supremacist march in Charlottesville, Virginia, in August 2017, Barack tweeted a quote from former President of South Africa Nelson Mandela: "No one is born hating another person because of the color of his skin or his background or his religion." This became the most "liked" tweet of all time.

Timeline

1961	• Born in Honolulu, Hawaii, on August 4.
1964	• Barack's parents divorce. He remains with his mother in Hawaii.
1967	• Ann Obama remarries, and the family moves to Indonesia.
1971	• Barack returns to Hawaii and lives with his grandparents while he attends high school.
1979	• Begins studying at Occidental College, Los Angeles.
1981	• Transfers to Columbia University, New York City, to complete his degree.
1982	• Barack's father dies in a car wreck in Kenya.
1983	• Barack graduates from Columbia.
1985	• Barack becomes a community organizer in Chicago.
1987	• Visits Kenya for the first time to meet his African family and visit his father's grave.
1988	• Begins studies at Harvard Law School, where he becomes president of the *Harvard Law Review*.
1991	• Graduates from Harvard Law School.
1992	• Marries lawyer Michelle Robinson.
1993	• Begins working as a lawyer in Chicago.

1996	• Elected for the first time to the Illinois state senate.
1998	• Reelected to the Illinois state senate.
1999	• Birth of first daughter, Malia.
2000	• Fails to win Illinois Democratic nomination for the House of Representatives.
2001	• Birth of second daughter, Natasha (Sasha).
2002	• Reelected for a third time to the Illinois state senate.
2004	• Elected as a Democrat to the US Senate.
2008	• Wins the nomination as Democratic candidate for US president.
	• Wins the presidential election.
2009	• Inaugurated as the 44th US president and the first African American president.
	• Receives the Nobel peace prize.
2012	• Reelected for a second term as president.
2017	• Leaves the White House after completing his second term.

KEY PUBLICATIONS
* *Dreams from My Father (1995)*
* *The Audacity of Hope (2006)*
* *Of Thee I Sing: A Letter to My Daughters (2010)*

Glossary

allies States that cooperate to achieve a shared goal.

apartheid Dividing a population on grounds of race.

biographies Written accounts of people's lives.

civil rights People's right to social and political freedom.

climate change Changes in global weather patterns caused in part by human activity.

deficit The amount by which the money a government spends is less than it raises through taxation.

diplomacy The conduct of relations between countries.

donors People who give money to a cause.

extremists People with extreme political or religious views.

global warming A rise in the temperature of the atmosphere.

inauguration The ceremony by which a president takes office.

keynote address A speech that outlines the key issues facing a conference.

memoirs An historical account based on personal experience.

mortgages Loans made to enable people to buy real estate.

nonfiction Writing that is informative and factual.

nonviolence Protesting through peaceful means.

primary An initial election to choose candidates for a more important election.

receccession A period of declining economic activity.

sexual orientation A person's sexual identity based on who they are attracted to.

special forces Members of the armed forces trained for secret and dangerous missions.

tariffs Taxes imposed on imported goods.

war on terror A global conflict with extremist Muslim forces.

Further Resources

Books

Hollar, Sherman. *Barack Obama.* New York: Rosen Publishing, 2012.

Obama, Barack. *Of Thee I Sing: A Letter to My Daughters.* New York: Knopf Books for Young Readers, 2010.

Torres, John. *How Barack Obama Fought the War on Terrorism.* New York: Enslow Publishing, 2017.

Zeiger, Jennifer. *Barack Obama.* New York City: Scholastic, 2012.

Websites

Ducksters
www.ducksters.com/biography/uspresidents/barackobama.php
A biography of Barack and information about his presidency.

Michelle Obama
www.biography.com/people/michelle-obama-307592
A biography and video about Michelle Obama's time as First Lady.

Obama Foundation
www.obama.org/our-story
A detailed timeline of Barack and Michelle's lives and achievements from the Obama Foundation.

White House Archives
obamawhitehouse.archives.gov
An index to the official archives of Barack's time in the White House, with many links.

Publisher's note to educators and parents: Our editors have carefully reviewed these websites to ensure that they are suitable for students. Many websites change frequently, however, and we cannot guarantee that a site's future contents will continue to meet our high standards of quality and educational value. Be advised that students should be closely supervised whenever they access the Internet.

Index

A
African Americans 10, 11, 12, 14–15, 20, 23
al-Qaeda 32, 40
apartheid 15
Audacity of Hope, The 25

B
banks 30, 31
bin Laden, Osama 4, 32, 33
Bo (dog) 35

C
Chicago 4, 12, 16, 18, 19, 20
civil rights movement 14
climate change 42
Clinton, Hillary 26, 30, 32
Columbia University 11
community work 12, 19, 31
Cuba 36, 40

D
Democratic National Convention 22
Dreams from My Father 25
Dunham, Stanley Ann 6, 8, 9, 29

E G
economy, US 4, 28, 30, 31, 41
global warming 42
gun control 36

H
Harvard Law Review 16
Harvard Law School 13, 16
Hawaii 4, 6, 9
health care 4, 23, 31

I
Illinois Senate 4, 20
Indonesia 9
Iran 36, 40
Iraq, war in 21
ISIS 40, 41

K L
Kenya 6, 9, 13, 16
Kerry, John 22
LGBT rights 38, 39
Lincoln, Abraham 24
Luo people 6, 13

M N
McCain, John 28
mortgages 28, 30
New York City 11
Nobel Peace Prize 32

O
Obama, Barack
  author 24–25
  birth 6
  childhood 8, 9
  education 10, 11
  elections 21, 23, 26, 28, 38
  farewell speech 43
  inauguration 29
  legal studies 12, 13, 16
  marriage 18
  name 8, 11
  second term 36–43
  Senator 23
  teenage years 10
Obama, Barack Sr. 6, 8, 9, 13
Obama, Malia 20, 34, 35
Obama, Michelle 16, 18, 19, 33, 34, 35, 43
Obama, Sasha 20, 34, 35
"Obamacare" 4, 31
Occidental College 10, 11
Of Thee I Sing: A Letter to My Daughters 25

P R
Paris Agreement 42
presidential elections 22, 23, 26, 28, 38
Robinson family 19
Robinson, Marian 35
Romney, Mitt 38
Rush, Bobby 21

S
same-sex marriage 39
Senate, US 21, 22, 23
social media 26
Soetoro, Lolo 9
South Africa 15

U V W
University of Chicago 18, 19
voter registration 20
War on Terror 32
White House 29, 34-35